Empowering Yourself Through Good Manners

Empowering Yourself Through Good Manners

Bernetta L. "Breezy" Watson

Library of Congress Control Number:		2011961719
ISBN:	Hardcover	978-1-4691-3036-1
	Softcover	978-1-4691-3035-4
	Ebook	978-1-4691-3037-8

To order additional copies of this book, contact:
Xlibris Corporation
1-888-795-4274
www.Xlibris.com
Orders@Xlibris.com
96390

CONTENTS

A book for preteen and teen boys on table manners, social skills, communication skills, personal hygiene, personal appearance, physical fitness and job interviewing skills.

By Bernetta L. "Breezy" Watson

INTRODUCTION OF BOOK

In every aspect of your life you will need good social skills, civility skills, communication skills and table manners and dining etiquette at home and dining out. Good manners last a life time.

Knowing what to do and how to do it can help you develop yourself confidence and positive self-esteem, making you feel comfortable in most social settings. Making it easy to interact with others. Rude and disrespectful behavior could keep you from having successful interactions with people.

Civility is courtesy, politeness, kindness and expression of kind words. Being civil is knowing how to treat others with respect. Some common courtesies are saying "please", "thank you", excuse me", "pardon me", "may I", and asking someone to be seated, holding a door for someone coming in behind you. Writing a thank you note, as soon as possible when someone has given you a gift or invited to an affair.

After reading this book you will have a basic knowledge and understanding of what it means to have good manners, making a good first impression, table manners, social skills, communication skills, and why it is so important to live a civil life style. Read, practice, learn and have fun learning new ways of how to be. Become a positive role model and leader and pass on your positive knowledge.

MAKING A GOOD
FIRST IMPRESSION

You only get one chance to make a good first impression. Impression is what other people think about you after observing your conduct and behavior. You will be judged by way you talk, walk, stand, eat, dress and interact with others, such as peers, friends, family, and other adults. Always be on your best behavior. You will need to be polite and well-mannered at all times, control your tone of voice and refrain from using foul language. Keep your body clean and your hair well groomed and your personal appearance neat and clean, make sure your clothes are pressed. Wear clothing that fit, no sagging pants, wear your belt. Wear socks and shoes that match your clothes, make sure all your colors are coordinated. Only you can determine what first impression people will make after meeting you for the first time. People will always remember their first impression of you.

First impressions are lasting. It takes 15 seconds to make a first impression but it may take the rest of your life to change a bad one.

THE MEANING OF GOOD MANNERS

Manners are social conduct and behavior. Conduct is a standard of personal behavior based moral principles. Morals are standards of right rules and knowing when to speak or to keep quiet. Manners are also using words like thank you, please, excuse me and you are welcome.

Greeting people with a good morning or good evening when you enter a room, a smile is always good it makes others feel good, doing acts of kindness for others and opening doors for ladies and girls. Let ladies and girls enter the door first. Help a lady or a girl with her chair when dining, pull her chair out from the table and assist her to sit down. Make sure she is comfortably seated at the table. You can also stand up on public transportation if there is no place for her to sit, you can offer her your seat. Good manners are from the heart. Living by GOLDEN RULE is the art of good manners.

"THE GOLDEN RULE" Matthew 7:12, what so ever you would that men should do to you, do you even so to them," taken from the KING JAMES BIBLE.

MANNERS AT HOME

Good manners at home begin with respecting your parents and all family members in your home. Follow the rules of your parents. Make sure you do your assigned chores in a timely manners do not let your parents tell you to do the same thing over and over do it the first time that your parents tell you, you will make life a lot easier for you and your nerves.

Help take the trash out, help bring the grocery in the house from the car, help your parents with smaller sister and brothers. Beware of loud noises you may play your radio or TV to loud. Come home the time your parents give you to be in the house do not make them worry about you always call if you are going to be late or your plans change.

Use good table manners at home and make sure to ask your mother or father if they need help in the kitchen. You can also help clean the table and the dishes after dinner. Be polite at home always remember to say please and thank you use good social skills and communication at home.

If you are having any problems talk them over with your parents do not keep them to yourself and worry about your problems making you rude and unhappy at home.

The most important rule and use of good manners and proper etiquette is please obey your parents and follow The Golden Rule, Do unto others as you would have them to do unto you. Remember to pray every day prayer changes things.

Have respect for others. Etiquette is a code of treating people with and making choices base on consideration, respect and honesty. Etiquette is about doing what is right.

THE MEANING
OF ETIQUETTE

Etiquette is a French word that means ticket. During ceremonial activities in the Royal Court of France everyone was given an etiquette (ticket). These tickets were the rules governing the Royal Ceremonies. The tickets let the people know what to do and where to stand in the court yard. They were not allowed to stand on the grass.

In 1750 the word etiquette entered the English language meaning a set of rules that our society wants us to follow. Etiquette is a set of rules and codes that society wants us to use so that we treat people with respect and honesty.

THE MEANING
OF FAUX PAS

Faux pas means a social blunder or social mistake or the lack of knowledge or awareness.

Example: To make an embarrassing remark about a person and you did not realize that the person was in the same room and could hear your remarks.

If this should happen explain your faux pas with grace, don't get upset just say in a clam voice "I am sorry that I made that remark or statement please accept my apology. We all make mistakes and it can be embarrassing, just correct the mistake and move forward.

There is one faux pas that we should never do and that is correcting someone's manners in front of others. If you see someone do something that you know is incorrect you continue doing what is right and they might follow your lead and good manners.

CIVILITY

Civility means politeness in a formal way. A polite act, acts of speaking kindly, courteous acts and expressions.

SOME COMMON COURTESIES

Opening a door for some one that is walking behind you is a kind and helpful act.

Saying excuse me any time you leave the friends that you are sitting with.

Saying you are sorry shows a concern for other people.

Saying thank you is good manners.

A smile and saying good morning is good and it makes people around you feel good.

Cover your mouth when you cough or sneeze. Make sure to use a tissue and wash your hands.

Do not comb or brush your hair in public.

When you have to pass gas, hold it excuse yourself go to the bathroom if you cannot hold it then let it out then be ready to own up and apologize.

Men and boys put down the toilet seat after using the toilet.

Men and boys take hats and caps off in doors, church, school, when conducting business, when visiting friends, hospitals, plays, musical concerts, and the movie.

No spitting

Be honest

Be considerate

SOCIAL SKILLS

SOCIAL SKILLS

Good social skills are getting along with others. The ability to interact, talk, listen and knowing what to talk about and which conversation to be a part of. Always remember to respect other peoples space by not standing to close to them. Do not touch people without their permission. Having good social skills mean having respect for others. Knowing how to conduct yourself in every aspect of your life in a social setting.

HANDSHAKE

The custom of handshaking goes back to early times in human history to a time of self-preservation when, according to the book, "The Custom OF Mankind" Copyright 1924 one savage fellow met another with whom he wished to be friendly, he held out his bare right hand the weapon hand—as a symbol, or sign, of peace—the other fellow understood—they joined forces hunting, eating, and probably living together in the same cave.

A handshake is the way we greet people in America. When we meet someone for first time we always shake hands and give a nice verbal greeting, like it is a pleasure to meet you.

When shaking hands, extend your right hand in a vertical position with your thumb pointing upward, and your fingers together, the web and index finger to meet the web of the other person's hand. Do not shake a person's hand to hard just give a firm hand shake, 2 or 3 shakes, let the person give a greeting before you stop the handshake. Always stand, smile, speak and make eye contact. Women, girls, men and boys shake hands the same way.

HANDSHAKE

A handshake is the way we greet people in America. When we meet someone for the first time we always shake hands and give a nice verbal greeting, like it is a pleasure to meet you.

When shaking hands, extend your right hand in a vertical position with your thumb pointing upward, and your fingers together, the web and index finger to meet the web of the other person's hand just give a firm hand shake, 2 or 3 shakes, let the person give a greeting before you stop the handshake. Always stand, speak and make eye contact. Girls, boys, women and men shake hands the same way.

You shake hands when:

1. When you are introduced to someone.
2. At the end meeting with someone.
3. After an interview.
4. When you meet someone you know and have not seen in a while.
5. When saying good bye to a friend or acquaintance.

This is how you make and introduction.

Make sure you always introduce people that do not know each other.

When being introduced

1. Always stand
2. Always smile.
3. Make eye contact.
4. Extend your right hand for a handshake, it is a friendly thing to do and this is the way we greet each other in the U.S.A.

5. Say something friendly like "It is nice to meet you or how are you doing?
6. Repeat the person's name.

INTRODUCING SOMEONE TO A GROUP

You say I want you all to meet James my next door neighbor, each person will introduce herself or himself.

RULES OF MAKING AN INTRODUCTION

Always introduce a younger person to an older person, say the name of the older person first.

Example: Aunt Ann this is my friend Jiamond, Jiamond this is my Aunt Ann.

You always introduce the higher status person first.

Example: Lt. Van, meet Sgt. Stacy, Sgt. Stacy meet Lt. Van.

ALWAYS INTRODUCE A MAN TO A WOMAN AND A BOY TO A GIRL.

EXAMPLE: Victoria this is Amos, my classmate, Amos this is Victoria my new church friend. Males always stand when being introduce to a female.

HERE ARE THE MOST IMPORTANT THINGS TO REMEMBER WHEN MAKING AN INTRODUCTION.

The most important person comes first. A person of greater importance would be considered such by rank, by position, by age (people having higher authority) or gender, in a social situation a women, especially and older woman's name would be stated first.

Example: Mrs. Obama, (important person) I would like to introduce Mr. James (less important person). You can add some background information this is a good way to start a conversation. When you make the introduction, say something interesting about the person, nothing that is personal or embarrassing.

Example: introducing a boy to a girl

Jazmine this is Troy my friend from school, his goal is to write a book. Troy this is my friend, Jazmine she goes to my church.

SOCIAL SKILLS
AT A PARTY

1. Arrive on time not early not late.
2. Find out what the hostess or host want the guest to wear, make sure you are dressed for the occasion and that your personal hygiene and personal appearance are just right.
3. If it is a birthday party, take a gift or gift certificate, a birthday card is good to take along with the gift.
4. Do not take another person if that person has not been invited, it would be rude to do so, because the hostess has planned for a certain number of guest, she has prepared a certain amount of food and beverage, there might be limited space in the party room.
5. Be polite and courteous to the other guest.
6. Introduce yourself, meet new friends a handshake would be a friendly gesture, with a warm greeting, like it is nice to meet you.
7. Use your indoor voice.
8. Remember to use your good table manners.
9. Have fun and enjoy yourself.
10. Leave when the party is over and it is ok to leave early.
11. Remember to say thank you to your hostess for inviting you to the party. You can also write a thank-you-note and mail it to the party hostess letting her know that you had a great time, do it as soon as you can, it must be hand written, no email or printed thank-you-notes.

SOCIAL SKILLS

Manners when you sleep over at a friends or a relative's home.

Always get permission from your parents and the parents of your friend before you stay overnight.

HERE ARE SOME RULES TO FOLLOW.

1. Be respectful of others
2. Use your table manners
3. Knock on closed doors do not enter until you have been given permission to enter the room.
4. Use your indoor voice (no loud noise).
5. Ask permission before you use the telephone or turn on the TV, radio or change any channels or radio station.
6. Do not ask personal family business and do not talk about your family business.
7. Please enjoy yourself but if you feel uncomfortable about anything call a parent and explain your concerns.

TAKE THE FOLLOWING ITEMS TO THE SLEEPOVER

1. Tooth brush, tooth paste and mouth wash.
2. A wash cloth, towel and soap.
3. Pajamas or sleep wear of your choice which could be a tee shirt or shorts.
4. A change of clothes, socks, shoes and underwear.
5. You may like to take your own pillow and blanket.
6. Make sure your parents know what time to pick you up and make sure your parents have the telephone number to the home that you staying overnight.

7. If there is a planned outing, like a movie, circus or ball game make sure you have spending money or this is a good time to use your allowance.

Please use good social skills, communication skills, table manners and remember your personal hygiene and personal appearance.

HAVE FUN!

INVITATIONS

When you are planning a party, invite guest in enough time so they can plan to attend your party. You should invite them at least three weeks in advance. You should send them an invitation or call and let them know about your party by telephone. When you send the invitation, give the time, date, location, and type of party.

You should have your guest reply back to you by providing them with a date to respond. R.S.V.P. french abrviation that mean please reply. You will see this on a invitations. Most people that are planning a party need to know how many guest are attending, so they know how much food and beverages they will need for party.

EXAMPLE OF AN INVITATION

You are invited to a party given by—

Date—

Location—

Time—

Type of party—

R.S.V.P by—

Phone Number 1800-200-8787

Ask for miss party planner

THANK YOU NOTE

Always send a thank you note for all gifts. You can also send a thank you note for a dinner invite or any acts of kindness. Thank you notes should be hand written. It is never too late to send a thank you note. Let the person who gave you the gift know how you appreciate the gift they gave you. Printed thank you noted are not accepted. Use plain paper or blank card.

COMMUNICATION
SKILLS

COMMUNICATION SKILLS

Being well mannered with good communications skills is not something you might think about having or doing, it is a most for your success in life.

There is no way around being well mannered, your success depends on it in your everyday and personal life as well as business interactions.

COMMUNICATION SKILLS

Being able to communicate effectively helps build relationships, leadership and positive self-esteem. Communication is a way information is exchanged between individuals through a common system of symbols, sings, or behavior or verbal or written messages.

Learning how to communicate effectively is very important.

There are many ways we can communicate.

1. Verbal "talking"
2. Signs and symbols
3. Listening
4. Body language
5. Reading
6. Writing
7. Computers
8. Cell phones
9. telephone

COMMUNICATION SKILLS

Verbal Communication

When talking to others always speak clearly so you can be heard and understood. Look at the person when you are talking. Be careful of how you respond verbally to others because you can never take an unpleasant word back. When talking beware of the tone of your voice.

When having a conversation with friends be sure to pick good topics to talk about. Do not talk about issues that will make you and your friends uncomfortable. If you get into a conversation learn to tactfully disagree and end the conversation. Cultural differences can get misunderstood at times.

Public Speaking

When you speak in public always know the subject matter that you are speaking about. Speak loudly and clearly. Make eye contact with your audience. You will have the opportunity to do public speaking at school, giving reports in the classroom and in church. If you belong to a social or sporting organization you will also get a chance to speak in public. You will feel nervous about standing and speaking in front of an audience. The more you speak you will develop a comfort level.

SIGNS AND SYMBOLS

When you see certain signs and symbols you know exactly what they mean. Example: when you see a red stop sign it means stop, a golden arch is the McDonald sign, there are many signs in sporting games that communicate to the people what is going on in the game.

LISTENING

Listening is a great way to communicate. Listening is to hear with thoughtful attention and consideration. When someone is talking do not talk at the same time, listen then make your comments. It is rude to cut a person off before they finish what they are saying, you can learn a lot by being a good listener. When you do make a comment on what has been said you can agree or disagree tactfully (without a argument).

COMMUNICATION SKILLS

BODY LANUAGE

Body language is an important communication skill, 95 % of communication is body language. Your body and gestures can tell people a lot about your feeling.

Example: Not making eye contact can mean that you are shy or not telling the truth.

Making eye contact when you are talking to a person is a positive communication skill.

Holding your shoulder's up shows confidence and good posture.

When you walk slowly it appears that you are lazy, walking briskly appears that you are confident and have a destination.

Arms crossed over your chest and hand's tucked inside makes you appear defensive and indifferent.

Hand's above the waist is positive. Hand's on your hip is a negative and a demanding position.

When both feet are on the floor we look alert and responsive.

When you are shaking your feet and legs it makes you appear nervous and less confident.

Fidgeting shows that you are nervous when you are moving from side to side when sitting in a chair.

When you are standing near or next to a person give them space, a forearm length away from the person. Stand eighteen to twenty-four inches from the person.

Example: when in a line at the store, bank, church, school, social affairs remember not to stand in a person's space, never touch a person without their permission, it rude and offensive to someone if you put your hands on them.

Now you can understand how very important body language is, people can read your body, so be careful not to send negative body language.

READING

Reading is a good communication skill, we read on a daily basis. We learn to read at an early age. We read signs, we read to follow directions on putting games together we learn to read to play games. We read the names of our favorite movies, TV programs and labels on foods. We read street signs, we read books for school and enjoyment at home we read our homework assignments so we can complete the homework. Reading is a skill that helps us learn to communicate more effectively. We learn to spell so we can read the better we spell the better we will read, the dictionary is very helpful in the correct way to spell a word it gives the meaning of the word and how to pronounce the word correctly.

WRITING

Writing is a good way to communicate, letters, invitations, thank-you-notes, books and newspapers. Thank-you-notes are always hand written when someone gives you a gift, invited you out to a dinner or allowed you to stay in their home. Thank you notes are personal and must be hand written and sent through the postal service not through an email.

Example of a thank-you-note, it can be short and sweet, not long and fancy.

To Aunt Ann,

Thank you for the blue necktie. Each time I wear it I will think of you. My new necktie reminds me of a tie that President Obama was wearing on TV last week. He wears the best blue neckties. I also have a dark blue suit that I can wear my necktie with.

Thanks, Nephew Tommie

THE COMPUTER

A computer is an electronic machine capable of accepting data at a high speed and showing or printing the results. This makes communication easier, faster and very informative many homes have computers, workplace, schools and colleges have computers for your use. Computer are the fastest form of communication we can get in touch with the world, face book, email and much more. Be very careful about the personal information you put into the computer it can cause a lot of problems for you in the future so use your computer wisely.

COMMUNICATION SKILLS

Telephone Manners

When you answer the telephone at home, greet the caller by saying hello. The caller will ask to speak to the person they are calling. Let that family member know that she or he has a call, use your indoor voice it would be rude to yell loudly to that family member that has a call. If family is not home, take a message, if the caller wants to leave a message. Write the name of the caller, number, time, date and any message. Give it to your family member when they return home.

Cell Phone

Cell phones are a big part of communication. Some parents provide their children with cell phones. It is a necessary form of keeping in touch with your parents, especially if everyone has a busy schedule. Cells phones are not toys and should only be used for important matters and only in places that allow the use of cells phones. Do not use your cell phone in school, work, hospitals, some public transportation and stores will ask you not use your cell phone when their service is being used.

BUSINESS TELEPHONE ETIQUETTE

There is nothing more frustrating than getting a call and not knowing to whom you are speaking to. Always start your conversation by identifying yourself.

EXAMPLE: how to answer a business telephone call.

Say hello or good morning or good evening this is Basic Chocolate Candy Store, Alex speaking how may I help you?

EXPAMLE: how to make a business telephone call.

Say hello this is Alex from the Basic Chocolate Store may I please speak with Mr. Payne? I need to make an order for 300 mini candy bars.

When answering the telephone in your place of business you should always be polite, use a pleasant voice, speak clearly and be informative. Always give your name and the name of your place of business.

The way you answer the telephone is very important. It gives an impression of your place of business. The tone, the clarity that you answer the call can be negative or positive experience for the person that is calling your place of business.

CULTURAL AWARENESS

It is good manners to respect people from different cultural backgrounds. A person's culture is based on and defined by history. Their culture is their belief in custom, religion, food the way they dress, the language they speak, and communication styles.

In the United States we greet by saying 'hello' and shaking hands. However, in some countries they do not shake hands, but might bow to each other. In some cultures, men do not shake hands with women. In other cultures, men and women do not sit together during worship service.

Today we live in a multicultural society. If you have a friend or classmate that is from different culture than yours, introduce him or her to your culture and he or she will share things about their culture.

If you want information about your culture, ask your mother, father, grandmother, grandfather, aunts and uncles. They are good at resource. It is wonderful experience to learn about another person's culture.

BEHAVIOR IN
PUBLIC PLACES

BEHAVIOR IN
PUBLIC PLACES

When eating out in a restaurant always use proper table manners, remember to use your napkin. Chew with mouth closed. Use your indoor voice talk about pleasant things make sure your conversation is good to talk about while dining.

Do not eat from someone else plate, ask the server for a small plate the food can be put on the small plate and then eaten.

If you have a need to go to the bathroom, just excuse yourself do not announce that you need to use the bathroom just go, always wash your hands before and after you use the toilet.

NEGATIVE GESTURES

walking in front of someone
cracking knuckled
backslapping
using toothpick in public
chewing gum in public
coughing/sneezing uncovered
checking your watch
interrupting
pointing
staring
whispering
fidgeting
laughing loudly

Remember to prevent negative gesture you must be thoughtful, kind, respectful, treating others with consideration. Rudeness is offensive behavoir, blunt or uncivil, impolite, uncouth and can make others feel hurt.

GOOD MANNERS AND COMMON COURTESIE IN PUBLIC PLACES

Excessive scratching of your head in public is unsanitary.

Laughing at others hurts their feelings.

Talking in church disturbs and it is disrespectful to other worshipers

Talking in the movie can annoy other movie quest.

Never point or stare at people.

Sneezing without covering your mouth is unhealthy.

Picking your nose is disgusting to others. It is unsanitary.

Picking at your ears is very unpleasant to others.

Yawning with your mouth wide open is not pleasing to anyone eyes.

Do not whisper in front of people, it might make them think you are talking about them it is rude and makes a person feel bad.

Gossiping is unkind and hurtful it is usually untrue.

How to treat people with disabilities

Please remember the fact that all of us are different.

When we see people having problems with the way they talk because of speech difficulty, do not make fun or a joke about that person it is rude, hurtful and disrespectful. Please be aware of the other person's feelings.

When you see a person in a wheelchair it does not mean that are not just as smart as you are, it means they have a physical disability and cannot use their legs.

You might see people with facial deformities, missing limbs, missing an eye, burns on their face and body, please respect individuals that have these differences.

They are just like you they have families and friends that love them, just like you. They go to school and work, and have goals and dreams, just like you. God loves them just like he loves you.

LIBRARY MANNERS
AND ETIQUETTE

Use your indoor low tone voice in the library, it is a quiet zone. Students are reading, studying and completing their homework assignments. There will also be library user that are there for the quiet atmosphere and the relaxation of reading a good book. You will find all types of magazines, news papers, CD's, Talking books and much more an example is the computer lab and you can get assistance any time you need help just ask a library assistant.

GENERAL RULES TO FOLLOW
WHEN USING THE LIBRARY

1. No eating, no drinking sodas or any type of liquids and no gum chewing.
2. No radios or noisy games.
3. No cell phone use.
4. Always ask the library staff to help when you need assistance.
5. When you check books out of the library, keep them clean and return them on time, if your book is returned late you will be asked to pay a late fee so always find out when your date to return your book or you can recheck your book out again if you have not completed reading it.
6. You can also check out movies and CD's.
7. You must have a membership card the card is free, with out a library card you can not check out items of any kind, you can use the library with out a membership card. The library can be fun, educational and informative.

CHURCH MANNERS AND ETIQUETTE

Don't worry about anything; instead, pray about everything; tell God your needs and don't forget to thank him for his answers. Philippians, 4:6

1. Make sure your personal hygiene and personal appearance are A+ when you go church.
2. Always check yourself in the mirror before leaving home for church. Make sure your clothes are neat, pressed and clean and color coordinated. Make sure your shoes are clean and polished, socks match your shoes and outfit. Your pants need to be pulled up with a belt holding them in place. Do not wear a hat or cap inside the church.
3. Always take your Bible to church with you.
4. No eating, chewing gum, no drinking soda.
5. No cell phone use turn your cell phones off.
6. No talking during church service.
7. No playing games or writing notes during church service.
8. Make sure you stay in your seat and not walking about while the service is going on, if you need to be excused to go to the men's room a usher will direct you in the correct direction to go.
9. Never walk about when the minster is praying or delivering the sermon.
10. When you accept an assignment like the praise dance team, choir, ushers or the youth group, be on time. Attend all meetings and practices if you can not call your leader and let them know that you will be late or you can not make it to the meeting.

MANNERS AT SCHOOL

1. Obey all school rules.
2. Arrive at school on time.
3. Go to your classes on time.
4. Do not miss school unless you are sick and have permission from your parents.
5. Turn in all your homework and special assignments on time.
6. Use your indoor voice in school.
7. Raise your hand when you would like to be recognized by your teacher.
8. Wear causal clothes to school always be neat and clean.
9. Be always aware of body and your personal hygiene, no body or underarm odor, take bath and be sure to use your deodorant.
10. Brush your teeth and use mouth wash daily before going to school so you can prevent bad breath.
11. Always have good manners and social skills on the school bus.
12. Do not chew gum in school.
13. Use your good table manners at lunch time.
14. Play fair on the playground with your classmates.
15. Always respect your teacher and all the school staff.

MANNERS AND ETIQUETTE ON THE SCHOOL BUS

1. Obey all rules on the bus
2. Stay in your seat until you reach school or home
3. No eating, drinking sodas or juice on the bus
4. No loud noise or loud talking
5. No playing around or fighting on the bus
6. No radios or cells phones
7. Obey the bus driver

MANNERS AND ETIQUETTE AT THE SHOPPING MALL

The mall is the place that some teen friends meet on the weekends to shop, have lunch and joke with their friends or go to the movie or play games at the game store.

1. Remember not to be loud use your in door voice.
2. When you go into the stores with your friend be respectful, no playing or eating in the store.
3. Do not play rough or run in the mall.
4. When you eat lunch with your friends remember your table manners and to use your napkin.
5. When you shop have fun while visiting the mall there are so many fun things in the mall.

MANNERS AT THE MOVIES

1. Follow all exit rules.
2. Use your indoor voice.
3. Take your seat.
4. Turn cell phone off.
5. No playing around with your friends like hitting, talking loud or rough play.
6. Do not put your feet on back of the seats.
7. When you are finished with your popcorn, candy and soda containers put in the trash can when you are leaving the movie theater, not on floor.
8. When the movie is over leave the theater quietly.

TABLE MANNERS

TABLE MANNERS

Just relax there is nothing that is difficult or hard about having good table manners.

You may feel uncomfortable and think you might embarrass yourself because you might not know which fork or spoon to use or how to hold your knife. After reading this book you will know what and how to do, use it as a reference book.

This book will help you build self confidence so that you will know exactly which fork or spoon to use and where to place all eating utensils after using them.

It is very important to have good table manners, you will be judged by the way you conduct yourself at the table and if you don't have good table manners you are sure not going to have good manners in other area's of manners. You will need to use good table manners at home, when you are eating out or at a friends house. Some job interviews are conducted over a lunch or dinner. There are so many occasions to attend social affairs where eating and using good table manners is very important.

TABLE MANNERS

Having good table manners are important; they are good social skills to have. When you have good table manners your friends will enjoy eating with you. You must use good table manners when you are eating at home, a friends house, or public eating places, or the work place.

Prior to beginning your meal, place your napkin in your lap. When eating, keep one hand in your lap and your feet on the floor so you don't kick the person across from you. Always use good posture at the dining table: sit up straight, hold your head up, and bring your food to your mouth.

Be sure to place small bites of food in your mouth, not large bites. Drink your liquids slowly in small sips.

The correct way to butter your bread is to break off a small piece of bread and butter it. You will have a small plate to put your bread on. Only touch the piece of bread that you will be eating.

When you are eating soup, spoon the soup away from you. Never blow your soup and do not make the mistake of slurping your soup loudly.

1. Never rest your elbows on the table while eating.
2. Chew with your mouth closed.
3. Do not talk with food in your mouth.
4. Do not blow your nose while others are eating; It could spoil someone's appetite. Go to the bathroom to blow your nose, and then wash your hands with soap and water to prevent the spread of germs. When you return to the table, do not announce the reason you left the table.
5. Cover your mouth with your napkin when you cough or sneeze.
6. Do not pick your teeth with a toothpick.

7. Do not spit fish bones or chicken bones directly on the plate.
8. Do not belch out loud cover your mouth with a napkin to stifle the sound, if belching continues, excuse yourself and go to the bathroom.
9. Do not eat off someone's plate. Ask for two plates, so you can divide the food and place on a separate plate.
10. Do not say that you dislike a food that is being served; just say no thank you with a smile and a pleasant voice. You don't have to explain.
11. Do say you enjoyed the meal to the cook, if you are invited to dinner at someone's home.
12. Do not correct anyone's table manners in front of others.
13. Use your knife when your meats needs to be cut also use your fork to hold the meat in place. Never cut all your meat. Eat the piece that has been cut, then cut the next piece.
14. When eating, place your napkin in your lap. If you need to excuse yourself from the table, this is what you do with your napkin; lay the unfolded napkin to the left of plate, place the soiled portion of the napkin face down.

HAND WASHING

Always wash your hands before helping out with the table setting and before all meals.

The proper way and length of time to wash your hands: you turn the water on to a warm temperature not to hot or cold, use soap, put your hands under the water, rub your hands together between your fingers, under finger nails and up to your wrist, then rinse your hands with water still running, dry your hands with a paper towel and turn the water off with the paper towel, then put it in the trash can. You must wash your hands at least 15 seconds.

Hand washing is very important in preventing the spreading of harmful germs that can cause illness.

THE PLACE SETTING

The way the forks, knives, spoons, glasses, cups, plates, bowls and napkins are arranged on the table cloth or placemat is called "a place setting".

The plate is in the center the napkin and the fork on the left of the plate, the knife and spoon are placed on the right, the glass is above the knife to the right.

BASIC TABLE SETTING

You will have many occasions to set the table. It's always good manners to offer assistance in setting the table. Always wash your hands before setting the table.

The plate of each setting is placed in the middle of the setting.

The knife is placed on right next to the plate with the blade inwards.

The spoon is placed facing up to the right of the plate next to knife.

The forks are on the left, with their prongs facing up.

The napkin is on the left or placed in the center of the plate.

Glasses and cups are placed above the plate on the right side, above the tip of the knife.

Your place setting should only be set for the number of people eating the meal.

HOW TO USE THE CLOTH NAPKIN

1. Place the napkin in your lap with the folded edges toward your knee.
2. Do not open your napkin on the table top. Unfold the napkin on your lap.
3. Leave your napkin on your lap until you are finished your meal.
4. Use your napkin to dab your mouth after eating or drinking a liquid.
5. Your napkin also keeps food and stains off your clothes.
6. When you sit down for your meal you can find your napkin in the center of the plate or to the left of the plate or displayed in a glass or on the plate, it is up to the hostess to place her napkins were she wants them.
7. When you leave the table to go to the bathroom you can place your napkin to the left of the plate or place napkin in your chair. Do not make a statement that you are going the bathroom, just say excuse me, it would be rude to say that you are going to the bathroom.
8. Never refold your napkin or place it on your plate after using.

TABLE MANNERS

Manners Do's

1. Wash your hands before eating your meal or before sitting down at the table.
2. Do wait for the blessing of the meal to be said before eating or drinking any part of your meal.
3. Use your indoor voice at the dining table.
4. Talk about pleasant things at the table.
5. Use your napkin, place your napkin on your knee, open the napkin near your lap not on top of the table.
6. If you sneeze cover your nose and mouth with your napkin.
7. If you leave the table, place your napkin to the left of your place setting, so that the soiled part is covered.
8. Use your fork, hold it like you hold your pencil.
9. Your spoon is used for soup, ice cream, Jello, apple sauce, and pudding.
10. When you are cutting your meat cut off one bite size piece, eat it, don't cut up your whole piece of meat.
11. When you have gravy break off a piece of bread, pick the bread up, use your fork, push the bread around in the gravy then put into your mouth.
12. Do pass the salt and pepper at the same time, even if the person only ask for one item.
13. When you butter your bread break off a piece of the bread, butter it eat that piece. Do not butter your entire piece of bread.
14. The correct direction to pass food at the table is to the right. When passing the food to the right the person can accept with their left hand.
15. If you drop your fork or spoon on the floor in a restaurant ask for another, leave the fork or spoon on the floor, if you pick it up do not put it on the table. If you drop your napkin you can pick it up.
16. When you start your meal use the eating utensils that is farthest away from your plate, first.

TABLE MANNERS DON'TS

1. Do not talk with food your mouth.
2. Do not chew with your mouth open.
3. Take small bites of food, do not stuff your mouth with food.
4. When drinking liquids take small sips do not gulp your drink down
5. Do not talk about subjects that will gross people out
6. Do not eat off a another person plate, ask the server for a small plate and place the food on a plate.
7. Do not put your elbow on the when you are eating a meal.
8. Do not wear your hat or cap when sitting down for a meal.
9. Do not kick the person sitting in front of you at the table keep your feet on the floor.
10. No singing at the table.
11. Keep your elbows to your sides while you cutting up your meat.
12. Dip your soup spoon away from you, do not blow your soup.
13. Do not blow your nose at the table, excuse yourself and go to the bathroom then wash your hands. You do not tell the other guest at the table you had to blow your nose, just sit down and continue your meal. It would be rude to talk to about you blowing your nose.

FOODS THAT ARE
DIFFICULT TO EAT

Soup; use your spoon, never slurp your soup, do not blow your soup, hold your spoon like a pencil and away from you. Never leave your spoon in a soup bowl, dip soup away from yourself gently scraping the spoon across the back of the soup bowl to catch any drips. Never blow your soup, do not place your mouth to the soup bowl bring the soup and spoon up to your mouth.

The reason that you do not leave your spoon in your soup you could accidently hit the spoon, and cause the soup to spill on the person sitting next to you, or across from you causing stains to their clothing that would be embarrassing. The reason for not blowing your soup is the same reason it could blow on the table or the person sitting next to you.

Salads; cut up your salad with a knife and use a fork.

Peas; use your fork.

Lobster; use a crab cracker and a cocktail fork.

Spaghetti; use your fork.

Eat Jello, ice cream and pudding with a spoon

THE FOLLOWING FOODS CAN BE EATEN WITH YOUR FINGERS

Bread, cookies, pizza, tacos, sandwiches, hotdogs, hamburgers, popcorn, corn on the cob, streamed shrimp, French fries, bacon, ribs, carrot sticks, chicken wings, chicken legs, celery sticks, pickles, grapes, apples, organs, bananas, watermelon, cantaloupe, chips, and candy.

PASSING THE FOOD IN THE RIGHT DIRECTION AT THE DINING TABLE

What is the correct direction to pass the food when you dining? Pass the food to the right. The reason for this rule is the great majority of people are right handed.

When you pass the food to the right the person can accept with their left hand and serve themselves with their right hand.

THE SALT AND PEPPER SHAKER

Do not reach across the table, do not stand up to reach the salt and pepper shaker ask the person sitting closest to the shakers to pass them.

The person passing the salt and pepper will pass both the salt and pepper at the same time that is the rule, it does not matter if the person only asked for the pepper you pass the salt also.

PERSONAL HYGIENE

PERSONAL HYGIENE

You must always keep your body clean, bathe daily or more if you play sports, exercise, run track, dance or any physical activities that cause you to perspire. Use deodorant to prevent underarm odor.

It is rude and offensive to others to have a body odor. Keep your body clean and dry and free from odor.

Always put on clean underwear and top clothing after bathing.

Every morning and before bed brush your teeth with toothpaste and use mouth wash. It is recommended that you brush after each meal but when you are at school or work it might be difficult. Make sure your parents take you to the dentist for your annual appointment.

Keep your hair neatly groomed. There are many hair styles, some teens wear short close hair cuts, locks, braids, twists, bush, long, or short. Keep your hair clean and oiled. Keep your nails clean and trimmed.

WASHING YOUR HANDS

It is always good manners to wash your hands before meals and after meals. It is also good manners to wash your hands after playing out doors and a healthy practice because you can prevent the spread of harmful germs. There are other important times to wash your hands before you use the bathroom and after using the bathroom.

HOW TO WASH YOUR HANDS

Turn on the warm water, apply soap to your hands, rubbing your hands together, between your fingers and finger nails for 20 seconds, then use a paper towel to dry your hands, use that paper towel to turn the water off, keeping your hands clean, put the paper in the trash can.

PERSONAL
APPEARANCE

YOUR IMAGE

First impressions are very important the way you dress can make a difference in the impression people will get about you. Present yourself positively by your grooming and your dress. You can wear a shirt, the shirt is wrinkle, your pants are not clean and pressed. You will give the impression that you do not care about the way you look or present yourself. Take the same shirt, it is clean, use some spray starch, press the shirt and pants, put a crease in the front of your pants. Make sure your personal hygiene is good. Shoes are clean and your socks are matching. You will make a positive first impression.

You might say, I do not know how to press my clothes or use a washer or dyer, I have a solution to that, I suggest you learn how to. Ask a relative to teach you or a girlfriend.

Make sure your clothes are comfortable and fit you well. Keep your style, do not compare your clothes to anyone else, you know what looks good on you. Set your own style and decide what makes you comfortable.

Your personal appearance

People do judge you by your appearance, I am not saying this is the right thing to do this is just the way society is. Making the correct choice about the way you dress is important. It does matter how you dress. Make sure that your clothes are always clean, pressed and fitting properly the length of your pants should be even and not sagging, showing your underwear or your behind. Hold your pants up with a belt. Make sure your clothes are color coordinated and your shoes and socks match.

Dressing for the occasion;

When you are dressing for school, movie, going out to the mall or visit a friend you should dress casual. Casual wear is slacks, jeans, shirt, sweater, tennis shoes, shoes or boots. When playing basketball, other sports and games wear your athletic wear and tennis and socks.

DRESSING FOR CHURCH

You can wear slacks, shirt, sweater, suit and tie or leisure suit. Make sure you are clean, neat and well groomed. You don't need new flashy clothes for church. Follow the dress code of your church or place of worship.

DRESSING FOR A FORMAL AFFAIR

When you attend a formal affair like a prom, military ball, a ring dance or any affair that the invitation states formal or black tie you will wear a formal outfit . . . If you do not have formal attire you can rent your formal wear from a formal wear shop. Making sure you color coordinate your choice of colors with your dates gown or dress color. Remember to purchase a corsage for your date make sure the color match her gown or dress. A flower shop will make the corsage for you, make sure you order in time and give yourself enough time to do all of this so you will not be in a rush and be late picking up your date. Find out if your date would like a wrist corsage, to be worn on her left wrist, or a corsage to be worn on the left upper side of dress.

This is a time that you dazzle your date, personal hygiene is perfect, hair groomed, nails manicured, haircut, shave and shoe shined.

Enjoy, have a ball and take pictures and please remember your social skills and table manner.

KEEPING YOUR BODY HEALTHY AND PHYSICALLY FIT

KEEPING YOUR BODY HEALTHY AND PHYSICALLY FIT.

Good health is very important. Health is the general condition of the body and mind, being free from physical disease and pain. Prevention is the key to staying healthy.

Keeping your body clean can help you stay healthy and prevent you from getting and spreading germs. Always wash your hands before meals, before using and after using the bathroom, after playing outdoors, or working outdoors. Keep your nails cleaned and trimmed. Keep your hair clean and well groomed.

In school if you decide to play a school sport you will be required to get a physical examination to make sure you are healthy to play the sport of your choice. Some of the activities that will help keep you physically fit are swimming, bike riding, walking, jogging, dancing, skating and playing sports and daily exercise.

Drink 8 glasses of water a day this will keep your body cleansed on the inside. Go to bed at a reasonable time on school nights. Eat less junk food and sodas. Say no to alcohol, cigarette smoking and illegal drugs.

Stay healthy and physically fit so you can enjoy life and a healthy body.

Dental health is also equally as important. Make sure you brush your teeth when you wake up in the morning and at night before going to bed. It is important to brush after each meal but sometimes it not possible when you are at school or work. Make sure you get your regular dental appointments. Make sure you cut back on the candy and soda.

JOB INTERVIEW

JOB INTERVIEW

You might ask the question why a job interview? Why can't you just go to work? This is the reason why, the employer needs to know what your work experiences are and if you are the person needed for the job. What is your general attitude, communication skills, your personality, your strengths and weakness, your personal appearance and your personal hygiene's the employer does realize that you are a teen and might not have a long work history or experience.

Take the time to write a resume', this will tell about your work experience. Some work experiences that you can list are all the jobs that you have had, like babysitting, life guard, helping elderly neighbors with yard work, cutting grass, helping with fund raiser for church and school. You might have computer skills, good communication skills with people and using the telephone. List your strengths and skills on your resume' with the dates and the length of the work experiences. You can list your references of your job experiences, with the address and telephone numbers so your perspective employer can get needed references.

When you go for your job interview remember to smile, make eye contact, give a firm handshake. Do not take a seat until you are asked to do so by the interviewer.

POINTERS TO HELP YOU NOT BE NERVOUS

- Locate the place that you are going to be interview a day before the interview so you will not waste time looking for the job site or getting lost.
- Be on time
- Do some research on the job you are applying for, have some knowledge about the business.

- Make sure you are dressed appropriately
- Take your social security card and resume' with you.
- Shake hands with the interviewer after the interview is over. Always write the interviewer a thank you note after the interview.

DRESSING FOR A JOB INTERVIEW

When going on a job interview you must look your best or the interviewer might think you really don't care and give the job to someone else that is dressed to look the part of the job.

The interviewer might think if you don't take your appearance seriously you want take the new job seriously.

You can wear a suit and tie to a job interview even if is not a suit and tie job. Wear a nice clean pressed shirt, white would be good to wear. Navy blue is the popular American business suit color to wear. You do not need to wear navy blue but please wear a professional looking outfit that is neat, clean and pressed. No earrings, nose rings, no lip rings, no tongue rings. No tattoos showing if you have tattoos on your arms wear a long sleeve shirt.

Make sure your nails are clean and trimmed. Make sure your hair is neatly groomed. Your shoes need to be polished and your sock needs to match.

ETIQUETTE CAN MAKE A DIFFERENCE AT A JOB INTERVIEW, Carol Kleiman, chicogo Tribune in a news article wrote:

"Etiquette is an important concept in a civilized society; It serves as a guide to manners and behavior usually in social situation. But what does it have to do with a job interview. A lot, your appearance, your manners and behavior and how you act during the interview, can keep you from getting the job or help you get the job. Dress for success, be well groomed shoes and sox should match, your hair should be neatly styled, make sure your nails are clean and neatly trimmed.

JOB INTERVIEW

Be on time for your job interview, being late might keep you from getting the job. Be well rested, alert, make eye contact, stand, smile, extend your right hand, give a firm handshake. When you greet your interviewer, introduce your self and make a pleasant remarks like it is a pleasure to meet you or it is nice to meet you. You will also give a handshake a thank you after the interview. Learn and know about the business and the job you are applying for. Once the interview starts stay positive, speak clearly, do not talk while the interviewer is talking, listen then ask question after the interviewer has completed his or her talk. Let the interviewer know that you are interested in what he or she is talking about all the information he or she is sharing with you.

INTERVIEWS

On the interview your appearance must be impeccable, meaning just perfect.

REMEMBER

Be on time. Locate the job site the day before the interview plan your travel time and your mode of transportation.

Dress appropriately. Make a good first impression make sure your clothes are well fitting and colors are matching. Your hair should be well groomed and your nails should be clean and filed.

Smile it shows that you are prepared for interview and that you have self-confidence.

Shake hands when you meet the person that is conducting your interview.

Eye contact it is important make sure you make eye contact during the entire interview process.

Do not take a seat until you are told to do so.

Watch your posture it is called body language a lot can be told about you by the way you stand, sit, walk, hold your head so please be positive, sit up straight, feet on the floor, rest your hands in a comfortable position. Do not crack your knuckles or twist your fingers.

Say thank you stand and shake hands after the interview

Write a thank you note your interview could be for job or to be accepted into a school.

THINGS NOT TO DO
WHEN ON A JOB INTERVIEW

People judge you by the way you look and dress. This might not be right but this the way people judge you even before talking to you.

1. Do not wear cologne that has a strong odor put on a small amount of cologne. Do not put the cologne on your clothes put it on body after your shower before you get dressed.
2. No visible tattoos.
3. No earrings or nose rings or tongue rings.
4. No hats or caps indoors.
5. No sandals or tennis shoes.
6. No sagging pants, please wear a belt.
7. No chewing gum.
8. No cell phones.
9. No friends.
10. No jean.
11. Do not talk about your personal business, stay positive.
12. Do be a good listener and pay attention do not talk while the interviewer is talking.

"Good luck"

LEADERSHIP

* To be a good and effective leader you must be well mannered have good communication skills be well groomed and most of all you must lead by example. Leading by example mean doing the right thing, having respect for others, being on time, keeping appointments or if there is a need to change the appointment call the person early to let them know that you cannot keep the appointment.

* A good leader knows how to work with the team, has good listening skills and willingness to work for the good of the team to accomplish the set goals.
* A good leader is a responsible person he thinks through problems and comes up with workable solutions that will benefit the team effort.
* A good leader must have strength and determination and have the ability to stick it out when there is a problem.
* A good leader has great organizational skills.

Every successful organization needs a strong, effective leader but the true success is obtain when the leader and the team work together.

The meaning of character

Character is the qualities that make a person who they are, their personality, their quality of mind, their feelings and their temperament. Character is also a person public reputation.

Making a good first impression is very important because this is the way people determine who they think you are and being truthful to your word is important and accepting responsibility, being on time for appointments is showing good character.

Good character is better than silver and gold.

The meaning of fortitude

The meaning of fortitude is having determination, strength, endurance, courage, stamina in a difficult or painful situation. A good example of having fortitude is sticking with a school class that is difficult and not giving up because it is difficult you can study more and ask your teacher for help, maybe you can get a tutor.

Fortitude is also being able to say no to someone that is asking you to do things that are harmful to you, like smoking, taking drugs or drinking alcohol and committing other unlawful acts.

Fortitude is being a leader and not doing wrong things just because your friends other people are doing these things.

The meaning of peer pressure

Peer pressure is social pressure on somebody to act, dress, talk, look like, behave or have the same attitude in order to be accepted as part of a group.

Never give into peer pressure, be yourself at all times. Never let anyone influence you in a negative manner to be who you are not. Beware of who you are and maintain your own style.

What is a bully?

A bully is a person that is aggressive who intimidate weaker people. A bully is a person who mistreats the weaker or nicer person. Children and teens are aware of bullies in schools and in the neighborhood. When a person is a bully it can cause pain and be harmful to others. Never allow yourself to be a victim of these mean people, tell your teacher, your principal, your parents. Never allow anyone to be mean to you or make you feel bad about yourself. You deserve to be respected it is your right and no one is better than you.

People that bully need love, understanding, friends, prayer and most of all they need someone to let them know that their behavior is unacceptable and cannot be tolerated.

Remember to keep your life in order.

1. God is first.
2. Family second
3. Next your education. A good education can opens doors for your success in life. In additions to your education you must have good social skills, communication skills, civility skills and table manners. You must have respect for others and live by the Golden Rule, "Do unto others as you would have them do unto you".